The Small Blades Hurt

THE SMALL
BLADES HURT

Poems by

Erica Dawson

Measure Press
Evansville, Indiana

The text of this book is composed in Baskerville.
Composition by R.G.
Manufacturing by Ingram.
Book and Cover Design: R.G.

The Small Blades Hurt / by Erica Dawson. — 1st ed.

ISBN-13: 978-1-939574-04-6
ISBN-10: 1-939574-04-8
Library of Congress Control Number: 2013955350

Measure Press
526 S. Lincoln Park Dr.
Evansville, IN 47714
http://www.measurepress.com/measure/

For Juliana

CONTENTS

I.

II.

III.

Beware of rashness . . .
— Abraham Lincoln, Letter to Major-General
Joseph Hooker, January 25, 1863

All goes onward and outward . . . and nothing collapses,
And to die is different from what any one supposed, and luckier.
— Walt Whitman, Leaves of Grass

I.

Layover

I've half a mind to make a move.

I stayed in Archer City where
I made Larry McMurtry proud
By downing one too many shots
Of ice-cold vodka, tumbler-sized.
I hollered every word of "Sweet
Home, Alabama" while the band
Reprised "Knockin' on Heaven's Door,"
Packed up, and quit the Legion dance.

I thought I didn't know that song.

I two-stepped with a cowboy, kissed
A Yankee (wrong), regretted it,
So found my cowboy once again:
The Yankee looking like a young
Paul Newman and the cowboy like
I'll bed you, hard and hot in jeans.

What was it in the Texas air
That brought Delilah out of me?
Was it the quail and wild hogs?
The BBQ cooked from a cow
That tasted like a slaughtered cow?

What hiked my temperature? It climbed
The diving board and took its clothes

Off, piece by piece, as if last May
Were my last picture show, last chance
To sweat with strangers in a Spur
Hotel room, quaint with double beds
And Byron on the table, me
As Cybil Shepherd in the lights
For the first time, marking the stage,
Walking in beauty like the night
Too much for such a little place
Where the town Indian said she
Was the town Indian; and, my
Sweet cowboy said I gave him eyes,
Said I was high-heeled trouble, said

I have the tendency to lead.

Rock me, Mama

I-65 has stalled. The spokes
Of Old Crow's "Wagon Wheel" have spun
The road enough. The singer tokes
And hopes to God he'll see his one

True baby tonight. The saga, sign —
The fatal bus crash in the '80s —
I'm not far from the Buckeye line.
And there's a milk truck and Mercedes

As Parks, from "Barstow," wants his bottle,
His twenties pissed — and me. I've missed
Another rest stop and the coddle
Of my own bed. My driving wrist

Cramps tight.
                    Pulled over at the Stop
'N' Go, I wrestle charring leaves
From the fog lights. Sizzling wings and, pop!
A high-watt beetle dies. In eaves

Of grave-like, ant-sandcastle dirt
I almost want to cross my chest.
          I wander through the mart and "Hurt"
In stereo, trying my best

To make it look as if I don't
Look obvious.
                    I pretend I'm light.

Shining in *People*'s blurb, YOU WON'T
SEE THESE PICs EVERYWHERE, the bright

Flash off a starlet's dress, a wink
Of black sequins until I dash —
Ashes. I ("...to a burning...") think,
What's with white boys and Johnny Cash?

And afterimages? Does no
One see essentially this see-
Me-see-me-not? It's like lotuses grow
Down south in blue grass — jujube

Served hot with eggs and all's forgotten
By noon. I am the lotus: mama-
And-baby soft, white bunny cotton.
I'm blooming everywhere to bomb a

Flat landscape, cover corn, shield herd
And house, and families dreaming of me
With a lullaby of every word
On the cd spun since Tennessee.

Some Kind of *–philia*

I am a suckerfish. I am
In love with my own mouth and one
Boat's balsa wood watertight hull.
I drink the Licking River dry
Like drought. I pour a 40 ounce
In tiny waterfalls for all
The fallen. I am pacing breath.
I am a riverboat's big wheel
Cutting through every wake's along.

The hull wants to be me.
                         I know
That it may write the waterline
But I'm all lip, rising something
Like a right-after-a-storm river
Swelling like it just up and died.

A Poem that's Not a Song or Set in the South

Maryland, my Maryland, a border line,
"Free State," disordered North/South, mountain pine
Cones west, bald cypress at the Bay, with brine

Along the coast and snow in Hagerstown,
White Oak, blue crab, orange and black, and down
The Ocean, *hon*, that January brown —

Do we even have a song? A soothing sound
Of the south? I want the taste, touch, wet mouth round
About the vowels in every guit-tar drowned-

Out syllable. My cousins have a twang.
I have a Mid-Atlantic pitch. Notes hang
Near a middle C. I say, *I'll do my thang*?

That just won't work. O, say, but can I see,
Say, quirks ("lacks natural lakes"), state oddity,
(One part's a mile wide) and sights (D.C.,

Where Lincoln's waiting)? In another place,
At the Potomac, dancing on my face,
A zephyr, boa-like, but commonplace

As my perfume, nuzzles against my chin.
Our Maryland version of a Chinook comes in,
Descending off the Rockies' next-of-kin

In Appalachia. Sing to me now. And wrap
Up all my naked skin. I want to nap
In its nook, wear its dress, and scotch its stocking cap,

Then follow it along to Arlington,
Another other place. There, I'd lie in sin
On soldiers marked unknown. The air is thin

And thick as if it offers up a cure,
A viscous antidote and I am sure
Of this "America in Miniature"

And anecdotes so much I know the pinned
And bowing Black-eyed Susans almost grinned,
Black-faced, enough to keep my peeled eyes skinned.

Speakers in the Devil's-Walkingstick

I need a piece of chicken.
Al Green is in the bush

Inside the mall. He's stricken
Me up. He's in the bush.

Outside The Limited,
Al Green is in the bush.

I heard him. Listen. Did
You hear the intro? Shush.

You hear the *I'm so tired
Of being alone*? Wait, there

It goes again. It's wired,
On cue, a jardinière

Rhythmic and blued. Al Green
Is in the bush. I want

To dance a Balanchine
Ballet. He's nonchalant.

He's attitude. He's smooth,
Outside, but limited,

Funky. I'll let him soothe
Me like an invalid

Who's got her legs back to life
Because Al Green is in

The bush like *Mack the Knife*,
Ready to cut the thin

World's rug, and turn it loose
Outside The Limited

Down from Charlotte Russe
Where every gothed-out kid

Smelling of kush can prove
His mama right and sing,
Won't you help me, pop, lock, move,
Cool, with that devil bellowing.

Listen. Al Green is in
The house. He's in the fizz

Of fountain drinks, the bin
Of half-off thongs. His

Voice is perfect. He's in
The devil's walkingstick

And on the mannequin
Who suddenly craves dick

Because the mall is all
Possessed. Each potted plant

Croons soul like it's a tall,
Black man who will enchant

The naysayers all shaking
Their heads, saying, "they're *always*

Dancing;"
                but, soon, they're making
Their moves through tiled hallways,

Saying, "my feet can't fail
Me now" since sweet James Brown

Can slide right in. All tail-
Feathers swaying *get down;*

Go to the bridge; stop; push.
This beat is like blackmail:

Al Green is in the bush
And there's a sidewalk sale.

Iguanas Fall from Trees

Like Hemingway House six-toed cats, sure-foot
Landings. They freeze for safety, freeze to warm
Until Key West warms up and all its put-
On masks for Bacchanal head in to swarm
The shops and Margaritaville.
                                    Cold deigns
To show its face, and when it does, it docks.

But it's only October. Buffet reigns
Under heat lamps. Palm fronds street-sweep the docks.
Winds fatten tee-shirts: Yeah, I'm old enough
To drink plus fourteen years.

                                    Let's move the year
Headfirst to January, all the stuff
Of winter. For our fake leftover cheer,

January, open. Spread your hand.

Catch me falling like newly planted trees
Fall. If you do,
                    then I can understand
Frail for cold's weight.
                                    Then I can feel the breeze

When I get up, just like the temperature
Rising like cresting surf before it's gone
Right back to lost at sea. You cannot cure
Instinct.
            The steel drummers keep playing on.

When Saw Grass Grows
to Meet the Sky

The Suwannee banks will boast forests of blades,
Serrated leaves, the steady bolsters high
And wading in the water. Carved arcades
Let August storms slip through; and, God, praise my
Lord, if the Tickweed bloomed, stigma fists to the sky —
Thief ants, weevils, and Green Fly renegades
Skim air like arrows. The wild battle cry
For what's way down upon the floor's stockades.

There let me live and die in riverbeds.
Thief ants steal food. Each Green Fly denizen
Defends dark blackwater. The Cardinal sheds
Red spikes before Autumn's pedestrian
Fall. Unseasoned and not, green strikes and clears
A path. Sharp dawn-to-dusk whetstones the shears.

In Celebration
of Black History Month

The early blooming Daphne is the best
Part for the black people in Idaho
If there are black people in Idaho.
And, winter moves, deciduous as rest.

And transitory as a breeze, the mouth
Of every wide pink bloom digests the air,
Its cold jet stream falling to grasses where,
Between the teeth, songs vibrate in the south.

Mojo like a Mofo

"And all at once my heart took flight."
— *My Fair Lady*

Now come on Dover, move your bloomin' ass.
How marvelous the ladies' necks don't break
Beneath their weighty Preakness hats. A speck
Of sweat. *Darling, your hankie?* At the pass

The Audrey heads turn right just as the lap
Relapses and the bear's on Dover's back.
Circling a wet morass itself, the track
Coughs mud. They're kicking now! The jockeys snap

The whips across the flanks. Penultimate
In the trifecta, Dover, go. Down front,
The heads adroitly grow to one high stunt
Chapeau with quill, petal, and parapet-

Like brim. Dear Ladies Baltimore, do we hear
The hooves' pursuit? Hear how they tumble, low,
Like final breaths of a real Pimlico,
Leatherhead like the horses' blinders? Hear

The dark-eyed junco in the neighborhood?
Hard knocks and circumstance mixed in the pomp
Of triple crowns and **PAWN!** Jackhammers stomp
Rhythms in asphalt. Know our Dover could

Be Pegasus, could leap the Mobil sign,
Leave Baltimore, our lips in Os. And noble

Equestrians could be, with all their global
Births, plain old jockeys working on the pine-

laced Anne Arundel lawns. The shadows loom
A step behind where, closing in, the seconds,
As hints of trace assume their place, are seconds.
The sod, mud, pass, and all the finishes bloom.

Oklahoma

I had half a mind for Richie Halverson
(And half for Tony Sims) when Grandpa shot
Himself. He did it in the golden haze,
Bright golden haze, right near a redbud bough,
Right when those two young boys swift-kicked my shins
Under the monkey bars. I swear the bone
Reverberated like aluminum
While rain rusted the roof's crosshatches. Two
Birds and a single stone, it's six and half
A dozen. I should have to know no more.

If only he had done it in November,
Beneath a redbud and bright golden haze,
When, like all romances, we'd all moved on
And that year's leaves were gone with nothing but
A carrion of branches strewn by hungry crows
Looking the least bit murderous. There would
Be nothing for the gun salute to hit
During the funeral, no life to bounce
Against, refrain, and no more boomerang
Of bullets spreading out its reverie.

The *click clack blaow* sounds like what dead sounds like
To children: tireless, meandering,
Unending like the sidewalk walk to school,
Littered with dormant zoysiagrass and white,
Thick boxes: hopscotch drawn with sloppy chalk,
Where a trove of worms gathers around a slug

Dying in table salt, like its twenty-some
Babies.

       If only it were February
When the ground beneath the snow's immunity
Has not one noise to mute. A winter sky
Could have had enough dark clouds to nigrify
My grandpa's morning black, or blue, to block
The sun, preserve the kind of haze where you
Don't know what day ends where or which one starts.
He could have slept while I outran the boys
And morning lingered in close longitudes.

If only we all lived in Oklahoma.

Who's dew to say that morning needed tears?
Time knows no hurt.
                  And who are we to say
The corn is not as high as an elephant's eye,
That all the stars aren't big and bright here, too?

Back Matter

This jigaboo moves here in shades of green.

I.

This version, 2.0,
Zion's bad seed, absurdity's
Daughter — I'm talking gangsta. Please.
I'm full of ghetto woe.

All you mamas cry. Please, call
Me too American, too black.
I'm gospel-singing with my back
Up to your front. I'm all

Go with my Nikes on.
Back: as in "go," sound on the tongue
Articulate, well-spoken, hung
In the aft of the mouth. Back: gone;

Arrears; to bet on. Back:
Pertaining to support; to cause
Backward movement; chillin', its hems, haws;
Brute force strength with no lack-

Luster effort.

II.
                    I do
It with my back into it, sweat

My skin, drug formicating, wet —
My fingers scratch it blue.

Hallucinations needle
The skin protecting them. I head
For the EMERGENCY — hot bed,
A microcosmic beetle

Of Cincinnati streets.
Pigs, no doubt, have a man spread-eagle,
Cuffed to a gurney, all the legal
Miranda wrapped in beats

Of EKGS, and blood,
(The point blank gunshot to the chest)
STAT angiectomy, last quest,
Red Jello gummed like cud.

III.

Back: animal; past due;
Belonging to a time like back
In the day — progress and growth both whack.
Back; backhand; and, a coup;

Defensive player who,
Behind the other players, scores
First contact. Back: as in watch yours.
Back: the body, new —

New emperor's clothes. Back: how
You know where you have been: Chi; Tao;

"Whaddup" and not *"goodbye"* or *"ciao,"*
But *"Peace"* and *"One."* *Back: now.*

IV.

Was I the once-green jigaboo
Who, now, sees red? Who, now, sees blue?
Is there a sadness close to true?
What hue is misery?

Can you see me now? I butt
In beats and flows and every nome
And phoneme while I'm going home
To lay back in the cut.

II.

I, too, sing America.

— Langston Hughes

I have a Mary Surratt-filled fantasy
With wood gallows but with no whips or chains —
Only makeshift handcuffs. Despite the three
Hanging, doomed men, I've got no time for pains,
Don't have the ear for her well-known last
Sentence of *Please, don't let me fall.* I think
Hanging will be a death something like classed–
up auto-asphyxiation: breath, a blink,
Perhaps the last; a naked corpse, a crowd,
Tickets even; a stage. I like it. I
Keep dreaming. Shackled, both our heads hang, bowed
And lady-like. We sing a lullaby
Like mothers, hers softer when the man veils
Her already-blackened face. White bag. One steep
Step to the drop. She falls. She snaps. She wails
Deep sighs like she knows she should be asleep.
I sleep deeply: her cradlesong is her neck's
Buckshot. Her head droops like a pheasant's. Smoke-
like dust, like ash, puffs up and bottlenecks.
When I'm awake, I feel she felt her choke.

Gave Proof

Before the Ravens came, we knew of grief
Already. We had orioles. We had
The Bromo Seltzer's light, and every face
Illuminating blue for twenty miles.

We had December 1917
And visitors rapping — at the front door,
The Baltimore PD in black on white
McCullough Street where Mr. William T.
Coleman was not to lay his hat. We had

Crow, gloating lamp-light and the gallant gleam
Baptizing the Constellation. We had one
Somniloquy of *We the people… We
Hold these… We, therefore… we been wanting…* We
Knew how to eat crab with Old Bay since that's
What makes it good. We craved Calliope
Whistles stationed in B&O hissed steam.

We knew the next cicada year would turn
Our nearby Sandy Point plutonian
Like last time. We knew snakehead fish would walk.

So, when the ravens came, Memorial
Was nothing: not a single wire. And all
The demons dreamed with open eyes so dark
They were purple. We knew that every heart's
Four chambers took the city's humid air
And grew denser, perfumed, salt-thick, unseen.

Florida Funeral

The tussocks grow up tall and June's hardcore
As hell. Storm winds heave Christmas palms. The fronds
Life raft along a squall. Mosquitoes soar,
Anhinga snake, runoff bellies to stagnant ponds.
The sinkholes never lose their quick. The sky
Disguises heat in dawn's abandoned rind.
Haze shadows everything. No wonder I
Can see humidity has left me blind.
It's been a minute since I've seen the sun
In lightning bolts impelling docks to sparks.
Each volt burns so I look at every one
And see a thousand lights in a million darks.
Burned. This is how Florida leaves me. I know
The reason why the river water stinks
Is its own weight, desire to overgrow,
Pervade the air, though the channel calms its kinks
And tides know some part of the day is low.
A gecko climbs, preserved in the veneer
Of oil. It's dead and, still, it seems to know
I've got to get the fuck up out of here.

What when the tussocks grow up tall enough
To cover all evacuation routes?
Interstates choke. I know I have to huff
The smell of grass mixed with decaying roots
Of jack-knifed trees. The too-wet soil heard
Danger and spills over when storms are tough
Enough to fuck me and the mockingbirds
Out of a flight. Sweet navels like it rough

And try to steady. I'm trapped as the twat
Of yawning orange blossoms opened up,
Unassuming, to the toxic paraquat,
Its caution streaks. Birds shit in a lily's cup,
June. My rills, too, are sick, June. When my skin
Reeks in its sweat, please do not make me claw
Out my own skin to find some air, June. Thin —
I'm a moment's wind simpering at saw-
palms. You've already made a woman out
Of me. I cannot leave. Your heat hangs hot.
Storms bury streets. I'm dead but not about
To die as rising heat prepares to clot.
Sinking humidity drops to the ground
And heats again. What when the tussocks grow
Thick and I lie in you to hush the sound
Of you, and that breeze comes back around to blow,
Just for a second, making me think I
Should move? I hear you. And I'm heavy, wet
Now. You cradle my head. You throw a sky
Dyed orange as the clouds begin to set.

Intermission

O Mary, don't you weep.
I got a primo seat up in
The mezzanine. Your song is sin
    It sounds so good, those sweep-

    ing hand snaps, constant beat,
The note that's in between the lung
And top of the mouth, right on the tongue.
    The bass doo-wops compete

    With *Martha, don't you mourn.*
The tan, humongous organ pipes
Tail up the walls. Their flathead stripes
    Make ceiling screws look torn

    As the Red Sea. Forgotten,
Mary? No. Your long note's the crown
Around the blighted army, drown-
    ded, a-singing *Mary*.... cotton-

    White conchs. You hold that note.
A million bones in water skin
Drift with your wakes. Seahorses spin.
    The stage begins to float

    Not to a climax hung
In sound still-life as dead as nature
But life in silent nomenclature.
    The treble S is slung

From the conductor's wrists.
There, in the faltering high C,
The alto's note, sad symmetry
    And syllable, subsists

    Like absent seagulls who,
Ashore, leave tiny fleeting prints,
As markers of their sustenance,
    And hover in the blue.

New NASA Missions Rendezvous with Moon

I. Pre-launch

Countdown: T-minus seven, six, five, four....
The camera's posed. The moon can cast its spell.
Right at the perfect time, the two will score
The evidential view: they're doing well,
Better together. Maybe now they'll find
The life source, water we all need, the sign
We should all be over the moon and grind
It out, rock solid, every night: resign
Ourselves to nature. At the camera's tine
And probing, the moon doesn't appear to notice —
Not taken off guard, not scared in all that dark.
You like a mission and a man. Play Otis
Redding's "My Lover's Prayer" to strike a spark.
Pray, *what you gonna to do tonight?* You've toyed
Where there is space. There is, no doubt, a void.

II. Contact

Where there is space there is no doubt: avoid
The physics, up the possibilities
Of failure. Once each atom, so devoid
Of size, swells with the charging chemistries,
(And vodka flows) there is no hope. You're screwed:
Inertia interrupted, senses dulled,
Intentions cheapened, school girl crush renewed.
In a matter of minutes, you've been nulled
To nonexistence. Now is not "before."
And details just don't matter: who or whom.
Countdown: T-minus seven, six, five, four.
Let in embarrassment and then resume
The mission. Success? Results too soon to view.
But where there's space, there is, no doubt, a clue.

III. A hit?

But where there's space there is *no*, doubt, a clue
Something's not right. Up at the moon's South Pole,
Right where the camera tilled, it's black and blue —
Space's unending shadow where the sun can't bite
Off pieces for illumination. And,
Up there, distance is short, inches not miles.
Try to see and not know where you'll land.
You'll find a crater near the rising piles
Of ice, water that lost its way and course.
How cold. -308 degrees.
The air is numb with possibilities.
The cold is bigger than the moon's own force;
And our survival hides in the craters' breadth.
Though, where there's space, there is, no doubt, a death.

IV. A hit

Where there is space, there is, no doubt, a death
In the afternoon, a pre-work fuck. You're still
In honeymoon-like heaven: heavy breath,
Body on body, energy to kill.
You watch his every movement, and his mission
Control. His muscles flex and slack and he
Chews plastic bottle caps. You are submission:
The Santeria smitten Shiva she
Who needs no sustenance, can walk on water,
Fly high sans happy pills, picture a white
Ball gown, *I do*s, the " aww" father and daughter
Dance, and the toast. You're dancing just as light
As Ginger. But, each mission is a tryst.
Where there is space, there is, no doubt, a twist.

V. Houston . . .

Where there is space, there is, no doubt, a twist
Of fate: Columbia, the Challenger,
Missions aborted, landing targets missed:
The universal principles astir.
Clotho, Lachesis, Atropos irate
Knowing how Centaurus, the constellation,
Is poised — all systems go — to obliterate
Dying white dwarfs or a nightly demonstration
Of how a cloud can just eclipse a star.
The moon eclipsed your world to *where'd it go?*
The moon, a stranger, sitting way too far
Away, unrecognizable, seconds ago
So bright, it's haunting: there, there, gone. It's stark
Where there is space. There is, no doubt, an arc

VI. . . . we have a problem

Where there is space. There is, no doubt, an arc
Of narrative: first there, then now, silence
And silencing progressions of the dark,
Away from missions with all the violence
Of smashing lips, clothes torn, legs splayed across
A naked mattress. This story is the land
Of climax, denouement, and albatross.
You've claimed your stake. And now, there is no hand-
Holding, and nothing speaks but a fountain's splash
Below, loud as moon-pulled tides clipping shores.
From lust and dust to dusty to flame the ash —
Your space is walls and tables, chairs and doors.
You did not know that it would come to this.
Where there is space, there is, no doubt, a miss.

VII. Re-entry

Where there is space, there is, no doubt, amiss
Or not, an optimism: future flight,
For mankind yet another step, the bliss
Of some uncharted territory. Night-
Eclipsing shadows never look to be
A saving grace. And now you have some distance.
Solitude's endless time becomes your sea
Of no tranquility. Rip tides, resistance.
Faint Venus, broken capillary Mars —
Fuck looking at the stars. Look at the hoar-
frost when winter comes back. Then, what was ours
Is yours. Your stomach drops. You wish your core
Was hot as the sun. You have a chance. No more.
Countdown. T-minus seven, six, five, four . . . .

La Revue Nègre

The curtain's up? Hey now! Away I go.
La vie en rose (ah hem), *Bonjour et O,*
Au Cabaret! (Look out!) Puccini's *O*
Mio bambino caro....I'll know
The other words then, too; sing Nina's woe
In her sultry old blue mood indigo;
With Johnny Cash, go make an Alamo
In Reno: we'll up and kill a man; I'll sow
Jimmy's cracked corn; and, then, Pinocchio
It: wish upon a star; I'll row row row
A boat; and, fit the battle of Jericho —

But, then, (Bravo!) I'll give it up and throw
It to my sidekick with the fine trousseau:
Ms. Josephine Baker — two woman show,
Expatriates, banana dances, "whoa,"
Revue Nègre, Nature's Black Pearls, *"Moi 'lo,'"*
"Don't Touch Our Four Tomatoes." We would tow
The audience to our private chateau
Brimming with leopards, liquor, curio-
Toucans, and every latest Romeo.

I've got to get a dog first, though, and grow
Pin-curled sideburns and learn to pose, tableau
Of taut breasts and the navel apropos
Of Paris nightlife, drop it hot, slow, low
As bass, tell Daddy Rice to tell Jim Crow
To take his minstrel smile and o-
pen up real wide to suck our titties. Lo,

How a rose e'er bloomed when you sang out, Sweet Jo.
You are our voice. Sing louder. Oui. Hello
And Enchanté. The bistro's spotlight glow
Will turn into a dusked seraglio
And crown us sultans. Yes, Madame Tussaud
Could wax us. Yes, we'll get some more Merlot,
Black Gypsy Rose. Don't stop your do-si-do.
Please flaunt your gold-chained hips. Work that bon mot
Banter. I'll make a keepsake video;
And, if you stop singing, I'll lip-synch, blow
A kiss to our United States below
The smoke that hovered with the mistletoe.

Tuck de Chilluns

— after Joel Chandler Harris

Clippity lippity, no, I'm not sorry, says
Brer Rabbit, running, gunning Fox's quest.
Fox runs, heads east, and gaining speed, heads west,
And hits his fox head on a hornet's nest.

The big payback — a doll, contrapshun, trick —
Brer Rabbit guns the Georgia road, all lip-
pity clip and drawling, *Mawnin'*, happy sans
The Doo Dah bluebird and the Laughing Place.

Brer Fox, all snuggly in the shadows' briar,
Watches his foe and his faux audience
Both talking loud and saying nothing. He
Can't stop his hi-jinxed days from going 'round,
Missing their senses, like contrapshuns left
For dead, all settin' there, the sky's black tar
Leaking off branches of loblolly pines.

Run 'long now, boy: Miss Sally callin' you.
It's yistiddy, already. Fireflies
Will suffocate inside those Mason jars.
A cow may need our hands for afterbirth.

Ain't got no time to sit mendin' our licks.

Chronic

I know the moon's persistent but a dead
Woman is rigor, more moonlight and branch
Than moonlight on a branch. I want to cut
My teeth on her. Her skin holds dawn's illusion.
Post-mortem piss dries yellow on her thigh.

I don't know why she dies or who she is,
Whether I murder her in quiet sleep
Because I can't dream dying, or because
I'm literary and need metaphors.

I do know moons are just a phase away
From their returns, and she is always there.
I've missed her more than enough to touch her in
What once was dew; hear her in rain that spits
Just like an ever-circling scavenger.

Night wears her now on its forehead in spots
Only a mother smells. There, in her rigor,
She smells of thunderstorms distilled in mulch,
Perfumed with petals closing moon-white plumes
To suckle honey — star anise, lime zest.

I sense her freesia in a zephyr's crook.

But I envy her night-blue artery
Looking hawkish enough to crack like hoarfrost.

Jungle Fever Epithalamium

Dearly beloved, can we call it this?
I've never left the States. We'll have the kiss.

The unity candle is just a guise?
Pronounce me wife, him groomed to colonize?

It won't happen like that. (So what.) He's white.
(Who cares?) I'm black. For me, a savage night

Is zigzagging, drunk, on a downtown street.
My hair is natural. I like my meat

Pink in the middle. Known to piggy back
July, I sop heat up like a biscuit. Smack

Is shit, shit right. Thirty and never caught
DWB, some random policeman ought

To let me get profiled.

                              Is it a yes?

I did know Randall Kenan, I confess,

Before I met him. (We still have those set
Meetings on Wednesdays.) I know I'd forget

When Dan clanned up, got him a kilt, and made
Us see those bagpipes if I could. (We paid

For that.) My god. When *Malcolm X* was ten
At the Cineplex, I read Haley, and, then,

Wore red and black and green — all proud, thick-skinned.
Mom said, "You know that you're from Maryland."

Is that a no, long-lost fraternal twin,
Black to my white? There'll be no Lohengrin

Chorus. No conga line. The rhythm will
Not get you. No. No dollar, dollar bill,

Y'all. It is not electric. Throw the rice.
Snuff out the unity candle. Let ice
Sculptures crack like the streets of Baltimore.
Bring on the wedding night. I'm ready for

The morning after.

                  Hon, hug out my spleen,
                  Crush all my bones. Position me and lean

My body up against the naked trees
Interred in summer love's transparencies

Drifting us through the threshold. Please. Unpin
My hair. I'm wild for your obsidian.

III.

In Black and White

Who else is really trying to fuck
With Hollywood endings, the clipped
Finish sealed with a kiss and dipped
In dark chocolate ganache? I've stuck

My hand into the bonbon box
Too many times. The Juliet
Costume won't fit my body, yet
Dear Romeo's a pair of socks:

One size fits most; and, we all die
So many times before our deaths.
I huff on all my last orgasmic breaths.
So, death, take off your shoes, stretch, sigh,

And take me from behind and check
The paw prints on my back. They'll climb
Away from you. There is no time
To mess around. Quick, clip my neck

With your grim reaper teeth — and, keep
Your hood on, hon — until we throw
Our costumes on the floor for show,
Expose ourselves as one big heap

Of bone and flesh and bone. With luck,
You'll clip me hard and I'll shout, *Dei,*
Ave Maria... and people will say
If it looks like a duck and quacks like a duck,

That girl's going to Hell. Please, can
I hold your scythe? And if I don't
Go to Hell, can you say it's that you won't
Take me. A spade's a spade. A plan

Can change. I love your pivot, covet
Your line, pin, point, arbor and shaft;
And I can dig it. Feel that draft?
Come close. Now tell me how you love it.

Ain't Got No Alibi

"I took thy sweetened pill till I came near . . ."
— George Herbert, "Affliction I"

Like love songs where the *you* is only *you*,
July's thunderstorm clouds are non-descript —
Just dark — and only there in that the view
Is that: a view. Some no name painter's dipped
Fan brush against a canvas that'll soon
Be blank again. Goddamn. I've just gone on
And described them, haven't I? Might turn the moon
To maple-slathered Sunday ham. Make dawn
Salmon. Shit. I ain't got a lick of proof
They're only clouds. Still, somewhere further up
Above the stucco, in the shingled roof,
I know a crack waits like an empty cup
For water. It'll land a tiny leaf
And turn into an ocean. What relief.

I'm talking nothings in my own sweet ear —
Like, maybe, you've lost it and split and this
Here's permanence. It's since before. This here
Is gone. Go on and get a big fat kiss
From Smokey's tongue; and, let her lick her wish
And whine her whine you're sure, if voiced, sounds like
A starving Oliver's "Please Sir." Her dish
Cries, "More." Outside, two big black crows lift, strike.
A hundred love bugs fuck in one big swish
Against the window screen. The swifts are yelling
For days-old bread and Darin's singing, "Splish-
Splash . . . on a Saturday" and Couric's telling

Us Elmo's full of lead. The crows holler ad libitum.
Nina Simone croons "I want more and then some."

And I'm dumb-founded when a day must come
Inside the shade-drawn windows where it's still
Nighttime and a pathetic mooning eye
In the moon. Winking, nodding, the moon is sly
As Charm City's sugary, cloying thrill:
A ***Domino*** when night falls. How the plum
Sky cries and calls to me in desperation.
You. Look. The stars suspend themselves. A cloud-
Crook capes my eye. Magenta shades ascend
The planetarium as storms upend
The sight. Every bright constellation's loud,
Insisting on disclosing its location.
The clouds, like bellies, bulge. Who knew
The eye needs light to see a glimpse of blue.

Chocolate Lincoln

"While soft falls the dew on the face on the dead."
— *The Picket Guard*, or,
All Quiet on the Potomac Tonight

If only all the dead had just one face
Carved out of chocolate, tempered and cooled, gallant
Collar and cheeks so perfectly caved I want
To lick them. If they could lie in state inside a case
In Adam's Morgan, they'd also know the grace
Whispered inside the hotel's restaurant,
The wine bar's wakeful nights, could call détente
After the President's prayer breakfast. Place
Means not as much as placement, though. The toll,
Collected, leaves the moving rich and the ones
Who moved captive, passive, and living caged.
Captain Lincoln, Caffeine Lincoln, a whole
Cacao Plantation Lincoln: in the sun's
Ageless tableau you're yoked to all wars we've waged.

Chinquapin Leaves
on the Riverbank

"Every one can master a grief"
— *Much Ado about Nothing*

I've half a mind to want it badly
Enough to tear the skin off my back,
And cut Mt. Vernon down to a stack
Of cherry blossom boughs turned switches.

Enough to tear the skin off my back,
The Potomac clinches, November cold
And cut, Mt. Vernon down to a stack
Of Chinquapin leaves on the riverbank.

The Potomac clinches — November-cold —
And its pillars stand tall with the swell
Of Chinquapin leaves on the riverbank.
Nightly, the district rights itself;

And, its pillars stand tall with the swell
Of every single monument.
Nightly, the district writes itself
Death and memorial clean slates.

Of every single monument,
I want its permanence and stone:
Death and memorial, clean, slates,
Bronzes, marbles I want to touch.

I want its permanence and stone
Everywhere I once brandished skin:
Bronzes, marbles. I want to touch
Cold surfaces and stroke the plain

(Every) where I once brandished skin.
A statue of what I was remains.
Cold surfaces and stroke, a plane
Descended space, hovering slow:

A statue. Of what? I was remains
And skull and slab, once. And I once
Descended, space hovering, slow.
I've half a mind to want it badly.

Rest

— *Picasso Print, Bagel Shop, St. Augustine, Florida*

I never saw the woman, just a bird
Inside the cheap frame's plastic glass. She hid
Her lips from me. Her face never occurred
To me. I saw a bird until black slid
Under its feathers, lifted them, and black
Fell from its mouth to another blackbird's beak.
Two birds. I wish I'd seen a neck and back
And breasts as red as a southern woman's cheek.

I can imagine this is how it feels
To love a woman. She stands, mornings, amid
The smell of homemaking, that quiet fizz
Of proofing yeast. She's almost there — a whiz
Of grounded wings spread in hopes to rid
Themselves of all the rest the dark conceals.

Everybody Down

Around this time of year, someone will fall
Over Great Falls. It could be me if I
Left Tampa's flatness for Virginia's drawl.
Altiloquent, high-flying cardinals' cry

Whit chew. The Civil War has its own app,
e-iPhone forts; but, love rides war roughshod
Over Virginia for lovers and sap
Sugar maples. I could get right with God

Here, and descend from blue preoccupations
Catching humidity latching on white
Oak trees, and tangle with indoctrinations:
Survival of the fittest; fright or flight;

Heat rising. Metamorphic slab for miles
Above the water table, stipule spines
Float somewhere for a stagnant spot. Rock stiles
Tease ticks to *Climb back up.* The ripples' brine

Is really schist's sharp grains. How do you like
Me now, God? Accident of fractured bone,
One with nature, the solstice, and a hike.
I bloom in spring. In spring, I die as stone.

Griot

Maw doesn't get that much attention. Boy
And Paw capture the white-robe spotlight, and
Even the other children Hayden leaves
Nameless. But, Maw is nameless, too. She's christened
By what she tells the children and her groom.
We baptize her as Mother, Wife, and South-
Symmetrical Maw. Is her drawl fog-thick? Does she
Sit by her man gaunt in his reek? Is he
Talking to her? Does she turn up her nose
At his hawked up spit and love him? I see her in

An apron, house shoes, with her hair pulled back,
With skinny arms, and hidden legs beneath
A long, blue dress faded from several washings.
If I could ask Mr. Hayden just one
Question, I'd ask, *what color were her eyes*
When you pictured her? And, if he'd tell me, I'd
Forget. I'd see each iris sinking deep
Inside her sclera, like the hollow eye
Sockets immersed in bone inside a skull.
Time was. Time was moonlight and sweetgum dark.

Little Black Boy Heads

Up at the top there lies a cowlick I
Just got to wrap my finger in, but can't;
Their cuck-a-bucks clipped down to the root; can't pry
One strand loose with a pick. Though I could plant
A kiss, perfect, on their round scalps' short threads
Like splinters on my lips, I'd rather fill
A field with a thousand little black boy heads,
Ascend a white oak high and stare until
Their shorn cowlicks appear to swirl. No hair
Would move, then one by one, the heads would tease
With growing spirals, hypnotize like air-
Embodied branches braced for lift-off. Please,
You stubborn noggins, take your hats off.
                                        Some
Day when I have my own, I'll palm his skull
And he will nap against my nipple. Thumb
In his soft spots, I'll sing of how I cull
Him from the black field bound beneath a sky
Bright blue, and sun so yellow the whole span
Splays green. His always-girl, I'll sing him, *Fly,*
Boy, fly. Then run away fast as you can.

If My Baby Girl is White

> *"only white,*
> *hair a flutter of*
> *fall leaves"*
> — Lucille Clifton

Mama says, What? goes outside and splits oak.
She brings the rope, chainsaw, and spikes — ties off
A limb. She takes the black tree down. The trunk
Breeds red heart rot.

                  It's too easy to say
It bleeds. Inside, the ombre fades from bark
To tan to thin white threads. Branches die-back.
The wood spews conk. The kindling leaves dark ash.

As unsound as a forest is, someone
Must slip and feel it. Someone sticks the dead.
The lightning bugs thud in their Smucker's jars.
Some mother, at the screen, must call, Light's out.

Langston Hughes' Grandma Mary Writes a Love Letter to Lewis Leary Years after He Dies Fighting at Harper's Ferry

My dearest, sweetest Lew —
It's like there's permanence in *West
Virginia*, not the state, the sound — the rest
After the *gin* fools you

And the *uh* goes on like "*Lee*"
And *autumn 1859.*
I've lost all semblance of "I'm fine."
So I say damn the free

Water beneath the thick
Ice spots on the Cuyahoga and Lake
Erie. Damn rifles. Damn the ache
Of numbness. Snowflakes prick

Your tall Oberlin grave.
I try to scrape it clean with my
Frost-bitten index finger. I
Marvel at how the cold can save

A tear, at how I sit
Under my chestnut tree and wait
For nuts, plate Charles' dinner late,
Allow Louise's fit

To last another hour.
Damn both my abolitionist
Husbands, their spot-on aim, fist-
in-the-air. Why don't they glower

Like I do when I yell
Louder than any choir could,
Or, out back, take an ax to wood
And wonder if you fell

Like broken logs, without
Movement, your body dead already,
All solid like a Cleveland eddy
The young ones skate about.

They're in love with being lovers.
The world's all to themselves. No sword
Can pierce them when they huddle and hoard
Their weapons under covers.

I wish them ill; no right
To do so, yes, I know. I'm so
Tired of when thin white sheets glow
Dusk red in autumn light.

Damn all Octobers, sin,
Forgiveness. Dam the streams until

Oceans of buried brothers spill
Like grief beneath the skin

Of rivers. Best intentions
And kind regards, Lew, take this letter
As proof I am not getting better.
I am its two-dimensions:

Two praying hands, my skirt
Pressed to my thighs pressed closed. Damn brass
Reverie and all the leaves of grass
So green the small blades hurt.

Ideation X

(I)

I'd give a fuck about the world outside
If Tennessee and its American
Holly swallowed me whole;

(II)

                      if Thuja Green
Giants would grow to armies, thick in toothed
Stinging nettle;

(III)

                  if banjoes reigned, string plucked
By plectrum;

(IV)

                  if the sky at Greens' View seethed
Nashville and boiled over;

(V)

                              if green plains
Curled with the breeze that wreathed white Skullcap grins.

(VI)

I'd give an arm for rye at 2 a.m.

(VII)

I'd give a leg to have my pulse slow down,
An eye to keep from crying, give this machine
Connected to my butterfly-pricked vein
If I could go back to my summer home
Where I won't dial 911 or hear
The plan to ship me down to Vanderbilt.

(VIII)

                           What if
My voice, all swoll' up in the chest, and broad,
Had said, *that box cutter you found was just*
For packages; said, *I agree; there will*
Be someone else; It's August; nine times three
Is twenty-seven; yes, ma'am: no, there ain't
No misery that's worth nobody's life.

(IX)

I wouldn't say I have a knife at home,
Nor would I swear I've often heard the cows
In Tennessee declare, *no more of your*
Imaginings. In Cincinnati streets,
I saw a brown calf chew on too-big cud.
I lifted up his ear to see the pink.
In Tampa, I am out for blood.

(X)

               If I
Could only find the means to watch the world
Implode — its red hot core naked, salt-thick
With blues — and, then, recuperate as if,
Like all of us, it has something to prove.

Acknowledgments

The author extends many thanks to the editors of the following journals where these poems first appeared (some with different titles and in different versions):

32 Poems: "Jungle Fever Epithalamium"

Best American Poetry 2012: "Back Matter"

Barrow Street: "Back Matter"

Birmingham Poetry Review: "Chinquapin Leaves on the Riverbank," "In Celebration of Black History Month," "When Saw Grass Grows to Meet the Sky"

Blackbird: "Gave Proof," "Langston Hughes' Grandma Mary Writes a Love Letter to Lewis Leary Years after He Dies Fighting at Harper's Ferry"

Connotation Press: An Online Artifact: "Some kind of *–philia*"

Georgetown Review: "Griot"

Harvard Review: "A Poem that's Not a Song or Set in the South," "Mojo like a Mofo," *"Rock Me, Mama"*

Iron Horse Literary Review: "Little Black Boy Heads"

Literary Imagination: "Chocolate Lincoln," *"La Revue Nègre"*

Mezzo Cammin: *"Rest"*

New Ohio Review: "Layover"

PoetryNet: "Oklahoma"

Prime Number: "In Black and White"

Smartish Pace: "New NASA Mission Rendezvous with Moon"

Sugar House Review: "Everybody Down"

The Book of Scented Things: "Chronic"

The Journal: "If My Baby Girl is White"

The Raintown Review: "Tuck de Chilluns"

The Warwick Review: "Florida Funeral," "Intermission"

Unsplendid: "*Ain't Got No Alibi*," "Speakers in the Devil's-Walkingstick"

Virginia Quarterly Review: "Ideation X"

The author would like to extend special thanks to the following:

Wyatt Prunty and Cheri Peters, The Sewanee Writers' Conference, and my whole Sewanee family; Paul Bone and Rob Griffith; Sherman Alexie, Major Jackson, Mary Jo Salter, and David Yezzi; University of Cincinnati, Don Bogen, John Drury, and Jon Kamholtz; University of Tampa, University of Tampa Low Residency MFA in Creative Writing, and Parker; my students, past and present; Caki, Erin, Carrie, Leigh Anne, J, and Phil; Dr. B, Dr. N, and Megan; Smokey; Stella; and, as always, Mom, Dad, Frank, and Mandy.

The Author

Erica Dawson's first collection of poems, *Big-Eyed Afraid*, won the 2006 Anthony Hecht Poetry Prize and was published by Waywiser Press in 2007. Her poems have appeared in *Best American Poetry*, *Birmingham Poetry Review*, *Harvard Review*, *Literary Imagination*, *VQR*, and other journals and anthologies. She lives in Tampa, Florida, where she teaches at The University of Tampa in both the undergraduate English and Writing program and the MFA in Creative Writing low-residency program. And she loves her dog, Stella.

CPSIA information can be obtained
at www.ICGtesting.com
Printed in the USA
LVOW11*0507120117

520698LV00002B/9/P